# WELCOME TO THE U.S.A.
# MISSOURI

Written by Ann Heinrichs   Illustrated by Matt Kania
Content Adviser: Lisa Weingarth, Information Specialist,
Missouri Historical Review, State Historical Society
of Missouri, Columbia, Missouri

Published in the United States of America by The Child's World®
PO Box 326 • Chanhassen, MN 55317-0326
800-599-READ • www.childsworld.com

Photo Credits
Cover: Creatas; frontispiece: Digital Vision.

Interior: Boeing Communications: 30; Getty Images/Allsport/Jeff Gross: 33; Getty Images/Stone: 13 (Frank Oberle), 26 (Josh Mitchell); Library of Congress: 28, 35; Missouri Division of Tourism: 6, 9 (Lake of the Ozarks CVB), 10, 17, 18, 21, 22, 25, 29, 34; Bill Naeger: 14.

Acknowledgments
The Child's World®: Mary Berendes, Publishing Director

Editorial Directions, Inc.: E. Russell Primm, Editorial Director; Katie Marsico, Associate Editor; Judith Shiffer, Assistant Editor; Matt Messbarger, Editorial Assistant; Susan Hindman, Copy Editor; Melissa McDaniel, Proofreader; Kevin Cunningham, Peter Garnham, Matt Messbarger, Olivia Nellums, Chris Simms, Molly Symmonds, Katherine Trickle, Carl Stephen Wender, Fact Checkers; Tim Griffin/IndexServ, Indexer; Cian Loughlin O'Day, Photo Researcher and Editor

The Design Lab: Kathleen Petelinsek, Design; Julia Goozen, Art Production

Library of Congress Cataloging-in-Publication Data
Heinrichs, Ann.
  Missouri / by Ann Heinrichs.
    p. cm. — (Welcome to the U.S.A.)
  Includes index.
  ISBN 1-59296-447-8 (library bound : alk. paper) 1. Missouri—Juvenile literature.
I. Title.
  F466.3.H453 2006
  977.8—dc22                      2005000527

Ann Heinrichs is the author of more than 100 books for children and young adults. She has also enjoyed successful careers as a children's book editor and an advertising copywriter. Ann grew up in Fort Smith, Arkansas, and lives in Chicago, Illinois.

About the Author
Ann Heinrichs

Matt Kania loves maps and, as a kid, dreamed of making them. In school he studied geography and cartography, and today he makes maps for a living. Matt's favorite thing about drawing maps is learning about the places they represent. Many of the maps he has created can be found in books, magazines, videos, Web sites, and public places.

About the
Map Illustrator
Matt Kania

On the cover: The Gateway Arch at sunset is a reminder of Saint Louis's place in history.
On page one: What a beautiful fall day to enjoy the Mississippi River and Missouri's countryside!

# OUR MISSOURI TRIP

Welcome to Missouri . . . . . . . . . . . . . . . . . . . . . . . . . . . . . . . . . . 4

Meramec Caverns near Stanton . . . . . . . . . . . . . . . . . . . . . . . . . 6

Fun at Lake of the Ozarks . . . . . . . . . . . . . . . . . . . . . . . . . . . . . 9

Branson's Silver Dollar City . . . . . . . . . . . . . . . . . . . . . . . . . . . 10

The White Squirrels of Marionville . . . . . . . . . . . . . . . . . . . . . 13

Historic Sainte Genevieve . . . . . . . . . . . . . . . . . . . . . . . . . . . . 14

Missouri Town 1855 . . . . . . . . . . . . . . . . . . . . . . . . . . . . . . . . . 17

Saint Louis and the Gateway Arch . . . . . . . . . . . . . . . . . . . . . . 18

German Festivals in Hermann . . . . . . . . . . . . . . . . . . . . . . . . . 21

Athens Battlefield and the Civil War . . . . . . . . . . . . . . . . . . . . 22

Bollinger Mill near Burfordville . . . . . . . . . . . . . . . . . . . . . . . . 25

Marshall's Corn Husking Championship . . . . . . . . . . . . . . . . . 26

The State Capitol in Jefferson City . . . . . . . . . . . . . . . . . . . . . . 29

Boeing's Air and Space Exhibit . . . . . . . . . . . . . . . . . . . . . . . . 30

Pet Tricks at Purina Farms . . . . . . . . . . . . . . . . . . . . . . . . . . . . 33

Tom Sawyer Days in Hannibal . . . . . . . . . . . . . . . . . . . . . . . . . 34

## FOR MORE INFORMATION
Our Trip . . . . . . . . . . . . . . . . . . . 37
Words to Know . . . . . . . . . . . . . 37
State Symbols and Song . . . . . . 38
Famous People . . . . . . . . . . . . . 39
To Find Out More . . . . . . . . . . . . 39
Index . . . . . . . . . . . . . . . . . . . . . . 40

Missouri's Nickname:
The Show-Me State

**R**eady for a tour of the Show-Me State? That's Missouri! You'll find lots to see and do there. Just say, "Show me!"

You'll meet Mark Twain and Harry Truman. You'll wander through spooky caves. You'll see white squirrels and take wild rides. And you'll watch dogs doing cool tricks.

Just follow that loopy dotted line. Or else skip around. Either way, you're in for a great adventure. So buckle up and settle in. We're on our way!

WELCOME TO MISSOURI

As you travel through Missouri, watch for all the interesting facts along the way.

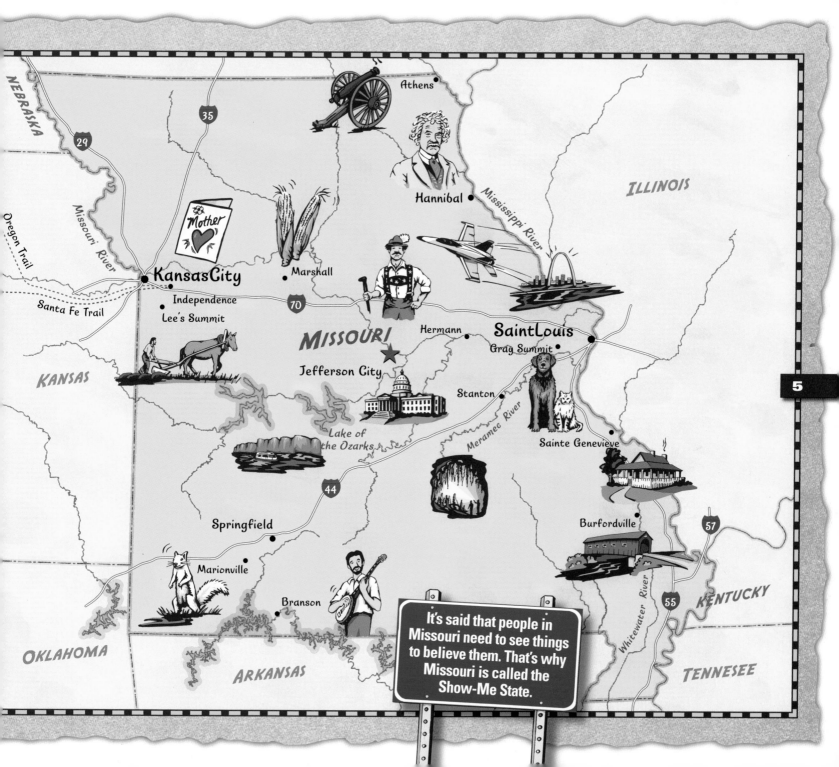

NEBRASKA

OKLAHOMA

KANSAS

Oregon Trail

Missouri River

Santa Fe Trail

**KansasCity**

Independence

Lee's Summit

Marshall

Athens

Hannibal

Mississippi River

ILLINOIS

Mother

*MISSOURI*

Jefferson City

Hermann

**SaintLouis**

Gray Summit

Stanton

Meramec River

Sainte Genevieve

Lake of
the Ozarks

Springfield

Marionville

Branson

ARKANSAS

Burfordville

Whitewater River

KENTUCKY

TENNESEE

It's said that people in
Missouri need to see things
to believe them. That's why
Missouri is called the
Show-Me State.

Tourists study the rock formations at Meramec Caverns.

**Harry S. Truman Reservoir is Missouri's largest lake. Lake of the Ozarks is the 2nd largest. Both were created by building dams on rivers.**

## Meramec Caverns near Stanton

Y ou're deep inside the cave. Awesome rock formations are everywhere. Some hang down from high overhead. Others reach up from the floor. They sparkle like jewels!

You're exploring Meramec Caverns. It's just one of Missouri's thousands of caves. They were carved by underground rivers. Missouri has lots of natural water springs, too.

The Ozark Mountains rise in southern Missouri. Many streams wind through their forested hills. Rolling plains cover northern Missouri. This is a rich farming region.

The Mississippi River forms Missouri's eastern border. The Missouri River flows across the whole state. It's the Mississippi River's longest **tributary.**

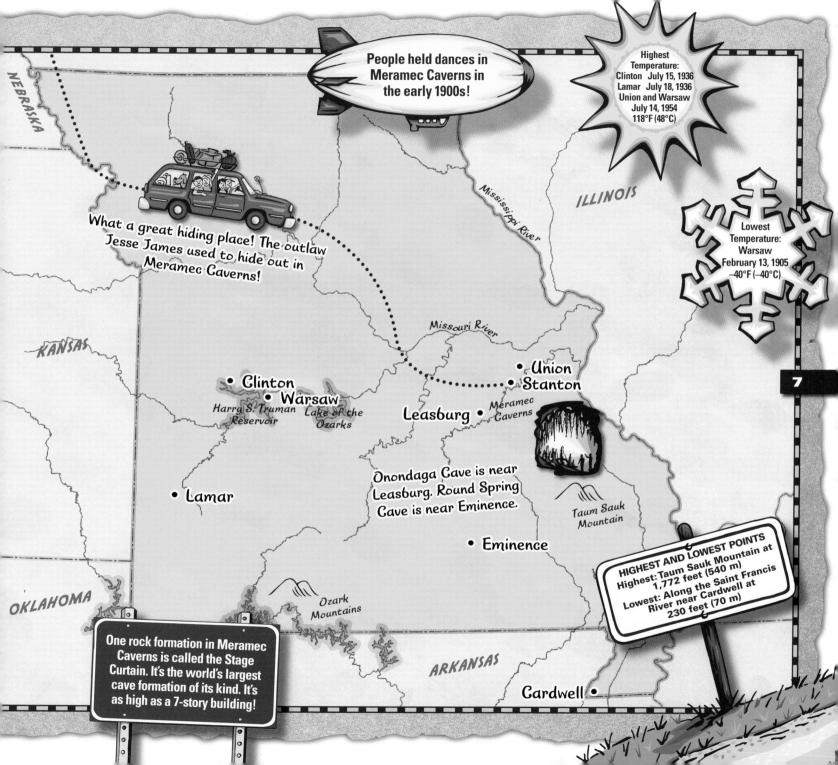

People held dances in Meramec Caverns in the early 1900s!

Highest Temperature: Clinton July 15, 1936 Lamar July 18, 1936 Union and Warsaw July 14, 1954 118°F (48°C)

Lowest Temperature: Warsaw February 13, 1905 −40°F (−40°C)

NEBRASKA

ILLINOIS

What a great hiding place! The outlaw Jesse James used to hide out in Meramec Caverns!

*Mississippi River*

*Missouri River*

KANSAS

• Union
• Stanton

• Clinton
• Warsaw

*Harry S. Truman Reservoir*    *Lake of the Ozarks*

Leasburg • *Meramec Caverns*

Onondaga Cave is near Leasburg. Round Spring Cave is near Eminence.

• Lamar

*Taum Sauk Mountain*

• Eminence

HIGHEST AND LOWEST POINTS
Highest: Taum Sauk Mountain at 1,772 feet (540 m)
Lowest: Along the Saint Francis River near Cardwell at 230 feet (70 m)

OKLAHOMA

*Ozark Mountains*

One rock formation in Meramec Caverns is called the Stage Curtain. It's the world's largest cave formation of its kind. It's as high as a 7-story building!

ARKANSAS

Cardwell •

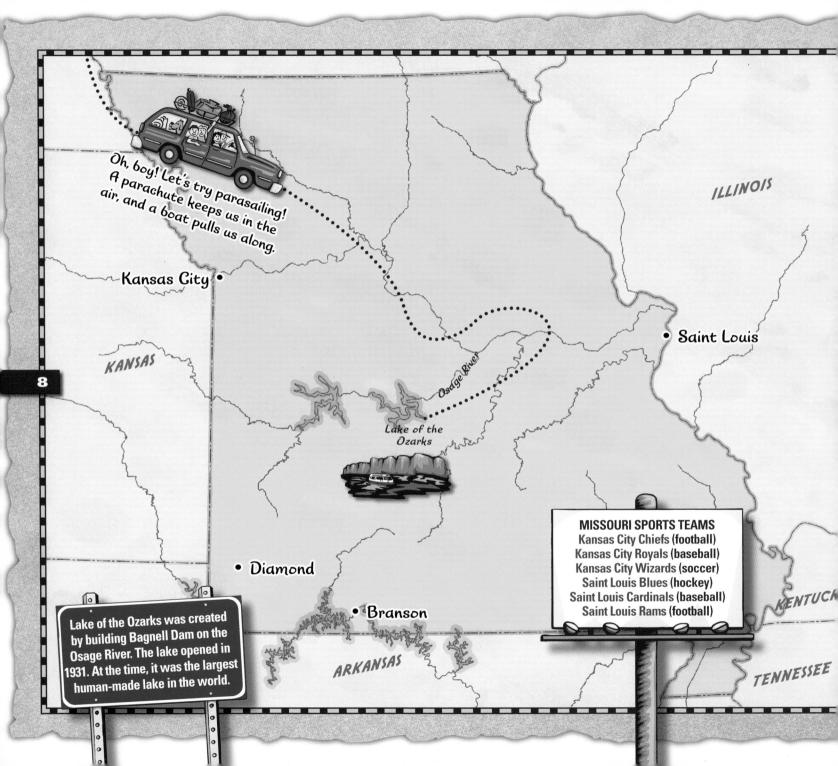

ILLINOIS

Oh, boy! Let's try parasailing!
A parachute keeps us in the
air, and a boat pulls us along.

Kansas City

KANSAS

Osage River

Saint Louis

Lake of the
Ozarks

Diamond

Branson

ARKANSAS

KENTUCKY

TENNESSEE

**MISSOURI SPORTS TEAMS**
**Kansas City Chiefs (football)**
**Kansas City Royals (baseball)**
**Kansas City Wizards (soccer)**
**Saint Louis Blues (hockey)**
**Saint Louis Cardinals (baseball)**
**Saint Louis Rams (football)**

Lake of the Ozarks was created
by building Bagnell Dam on the
Osage River. The lake opened in
1931. At the time, it was the largest
human-made lake in the world.

## Fun at Lake of the Ozarks

**Z**oom around the lake in a boat. Speed along on water skis. Go swimming or fishing. Or just be lazy and sunbathe. You're enjoying Lake of the Ozarks!

This huge lake is a popular vacation spot. Some people enjoy the Ozarks' forests and streams. They like hiking, camping, and watching wildlife.

Country-music fans head for Branson. It has dozens of music theaters. Silver Dollar City is in Branson, too. It's a theme park with crafts, rides, and shows.

Missouri also has many museums and historic sites. Its sports teams draw big crowds, too. Whatever you enjoy, you'll find it in Missouri!

Grab your sunscreen! It's time to take a boat trip on Lake of the Ozarks!

George Washington Carver was an African American scientist. He developed many new farm products. His birthplace near Diamond is a national monument.

## Branson's Silver Dollar City

Splash! Visitors to Silver Dollar City ride the American Plunge.

Silver Dollar City developed around Marvel Cave. It's Missouri's deepest cave. Visitors to the park can tour the cave.

**Y**ou could spend days at Silver Dollar City! It's built like an old Ozarks mining town. Stroll around the theme park. You'll see people working on pioneer crafts. Some are blowing glass or making pottery. Some are making candy or candles. You'll see blacksmiths and wood-carvers, too.

Maybe you'd like the rides. Try the American Plunge. You drop down five stories and get splashed. Do you really want to get wet? Then twist and turn on the WaterWorks Waterboggan.

Geyser Gulch might be your style. This giant playground is the world's largest tree house. Or ride the Frisco Steam Train. Watch out, though. Some crazy train robbers will jump on!

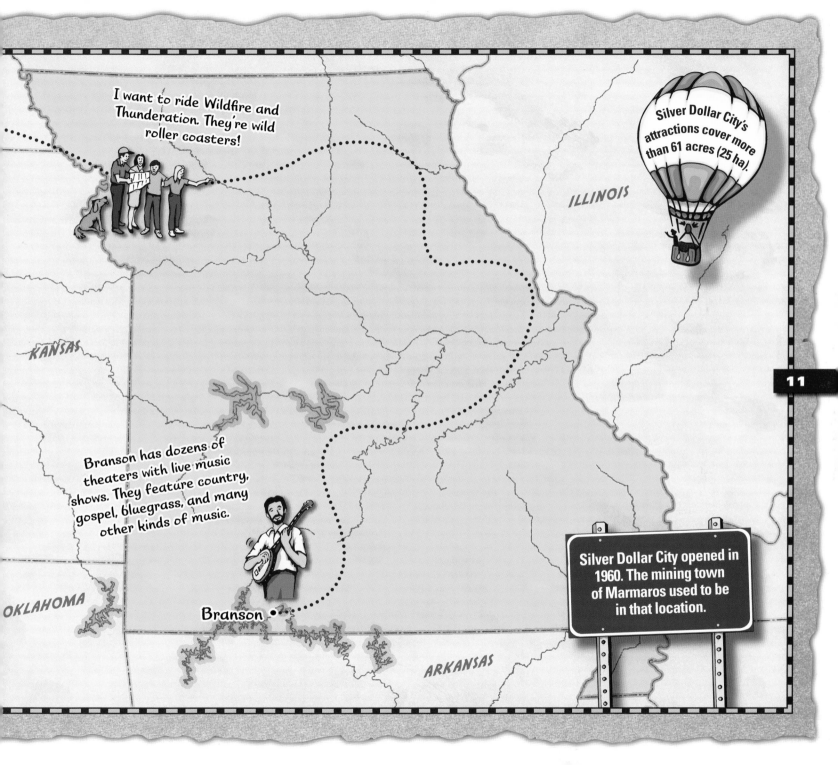

I want to ride Wildfire and Thunderation. They're wild roller coasters!

Silver Dollar City's attractions cover more than 61 acres (25 ha).

ILLINOIS

KANSAS

Branson has dozens of theaters with live music shows. They feature country, gospel, bluegrass, and many other kinds of music.

Silver Dollar City opened in 1960. The mining town of Marmaros used to be in that location.

OKLAHOMA

Branson

ARKANSAS

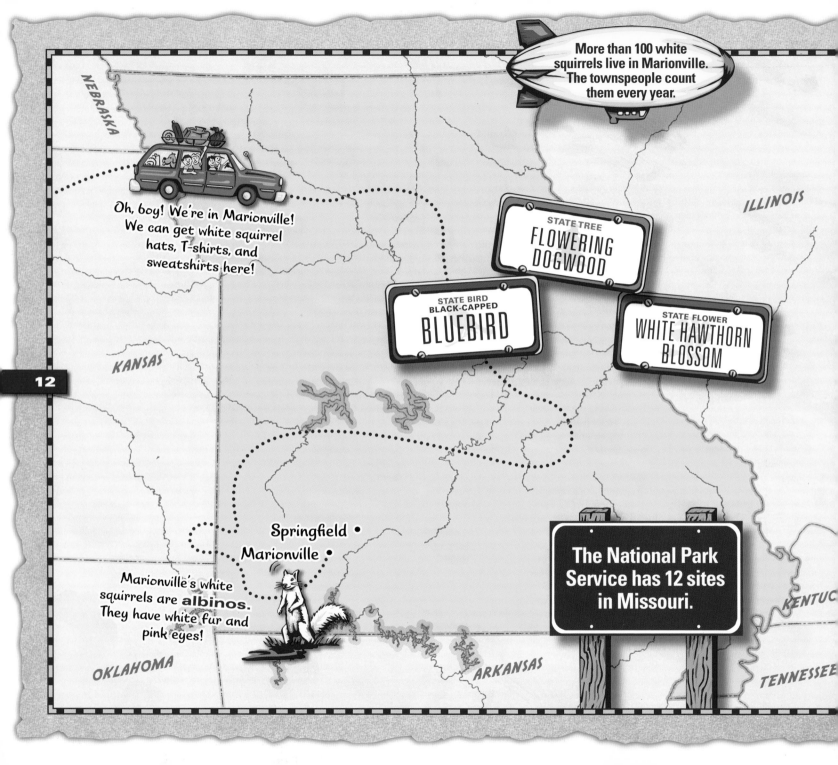

More than 100 white squirrels live in Marionville. The townspeople count them every year.

Oh, boy! We're in Marionville! We can get white squirrel hats, T-shirts, and sweatshirts here!

STATE TREE
FLOWERING DOGWOOD

STATE BIRD
BLACK-CAPPED
BLUEBIRD

STATE FLOWER
WHITE HAWTHORN BLOSSOM

Springfield •
Marionville •

Marionville's white squirrels are **albinos**. They have white fur and pink eyes!

The National Park Service has 12 sites in Missouri.

NEBRASKA

ILLINOIS

KANSAS

OKLAHOMA

ARKANSAS

KENTUC

TENNESSE

## The White Squirrels of Marionville

This fawn makes its home on Missouri's prairie.

**S**omething white and furry scurries across the park. What can it be? If you're in Marionville, it's a white squirrel!

Marionville is famous for its white squirrels. They eat corn, nuts, and sunflower seeds. Try being really quiet and still. They may take food from your hand!

Most of Missouri's squirrels are gray. They live wherever there are lots of trees. Forests in the Ozarks are home to many animals. Deer are the biggest of them. Smaller animals include skunks, beavers, foxes, and rabbits. Quails live mostly on the ground. These birds are sometimes called bobwhites. That's because their call sounds like "bob-white!"

Ozark Cavefish National Wildlife Refuge is west of Springfield in Lawrence County. It protects the Ozark cavefish. This blind fish lives in a stream within a cave.

## Historic Sainte Genevieve

Strike up a tune! Enjoy the music at Sainte Genevieve's French Heritage Festival.

**Pierre Laclède founded Saint Louis in 1764. He was a French fur trader.**

**S**top by Sainte Genevieve's French **Heritage** Festival. You'll see folk dancers kicking up their heels. French folk songs fill the air. Townspeople are acting out historic events. And they're all dressed in old French costumes.

Sainte Genevieve is Missouri's oldest city. French people founded it in 1735.

French explorers were the first Europeans in Missouri. Those explorers originally went to Canada. Then they sailed down the Mississippi River to Missouri. There they met many American Indians.

French fur traders set up trading posts. They traded with the Indians for furs. French **missionaries** came, too. They taught Christianity to the Indians.

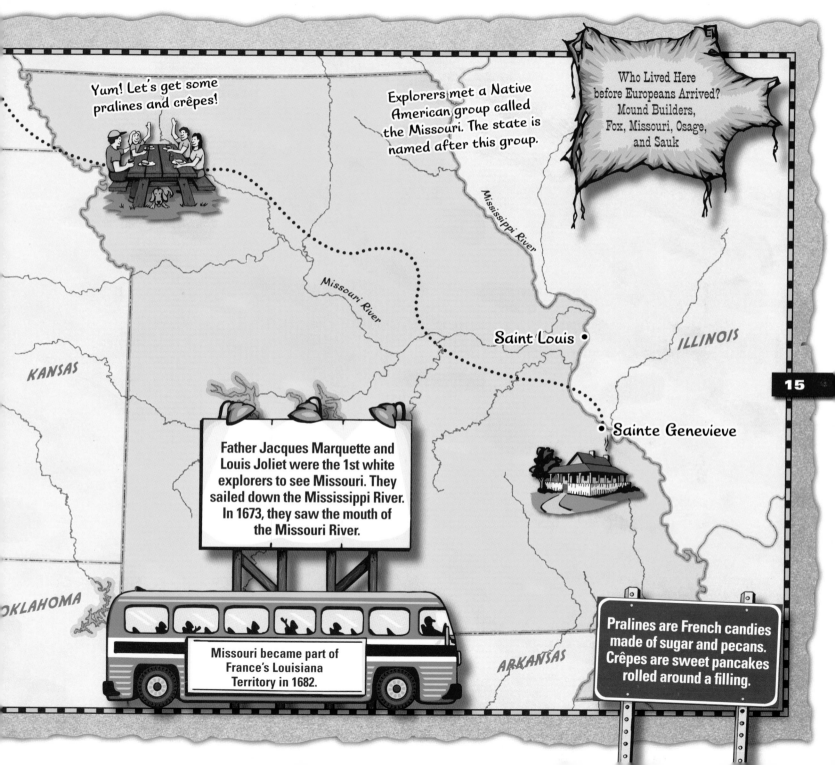

Yum! Let's get some pralines and crêpes!

Explorers met a Native American group called the Missouri. The state is named after this group.

Who Lived Here before Europeans Arrived? Mound Builders, Fox, Missouri, Osage, and Sauk

Mississippi River

Missouri River

Saint Louis •

ILLINOIS

• Sainte Genevieve

KANSAS

Father Jacques Marquette and Louis Joliet were the 1st white explorers to see Missouri. They sailed down the Mississippi River. In 1673, they saw the mouth of the Missouri River.

OKLAHOMA

Missouri became part of France's Louisiana Territory in 1682.

ARKANSAS

Pralines are French candies made of sugar and pecans. Crêpes are sweet pancakes rolled around a filling.

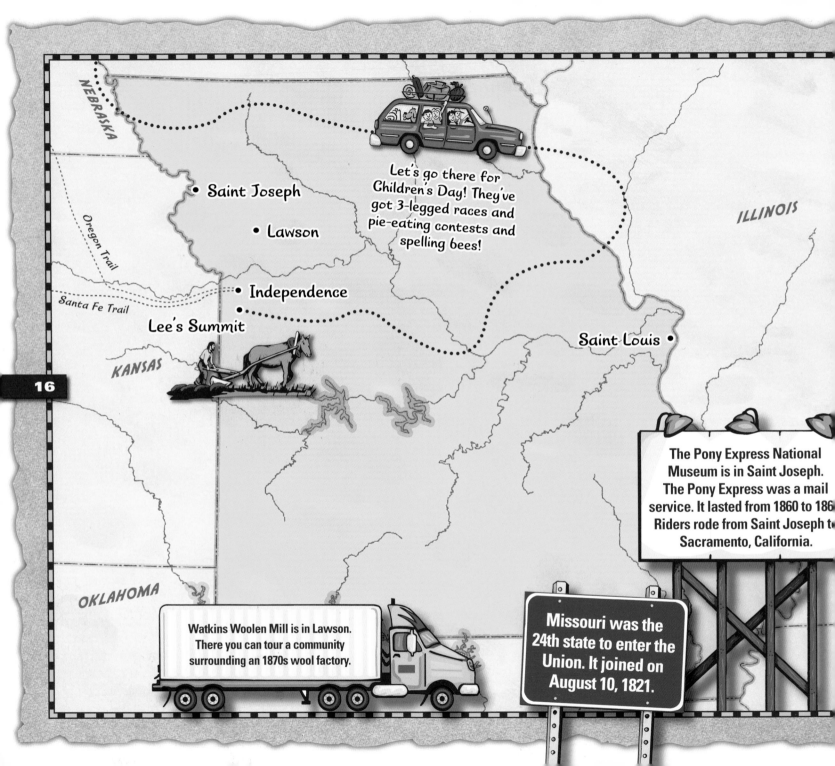

NEBRASKA

Saint Joseph

Lawson

Oregon Trail

Santa Fe Trail

Independence

Lee's Summit

KANSAS

OKLAHOMA

ILLINOIS

Saint Louis

Let's go there for Children's Day! They've got 3-legged races and pie-eating contests and spelling bees!

The Pony Express National Museum is in Saint Joseph. The Pony Express was a mail service. It lasted from 1860 to 186[ ] Riders rode from Saint Joseph t[ ] Sacramento, California.

Watkins Woolen Mill is in Lawson. There you can tour a community surrounding an 1870s wool factory.

Missouri was the 24th state to enter the Union. It joined on August 10, 1821.

# Missouri Town 1855

The United States gained Missouri in 1803. No one knew much about lands farther west. Meriwether Lewis and William Clark explored those lands. They set out from Saint Louis in 1804.

Soon settlers began farming in Missouri. Want to see how they lived? Just visit Missouri Town 1855. It's near Lee's Summit. People there are dressed in 1800s outfits. They're doing farm chores and other daily activities. They explain their work. And you can pet the farm animals!

Thousands of **pioneers** headed west from Missouri. They took the Santa Fe and Oregon trails. Both of these trails began in Independence.

Have you traveled back to 1855? No, you're just watching actors at Missouri Town.

The National Frontier Trails Center is in Independence. There you'll learn all about the trails pioneers took west.

Want the best view of Saint Louis? Ride to the top of the Gateway Arch!

The International Bowling Museum is in Saint Louis.

## Saint Louis and the Gateway Arch

Ride to the top of the Gateway **Arch.** It's taller than two Statues of Liberty! Look around, and you'll see awesome views. Does it feel like the arch is moving? Don't worry. It's built to sway in the wind!

Saint Louis is called the Gateway to the West. Many pioneers began traveling west from there. That's how the Gateway Arch got its name.

Saint Louis has many fun places to visit. You'll see animal shows at the city's zoo. Then explore the Saint Louis Science Center. You can try digging for dinosaur bones there! The city has many other museums and parks. Take time to see them all!

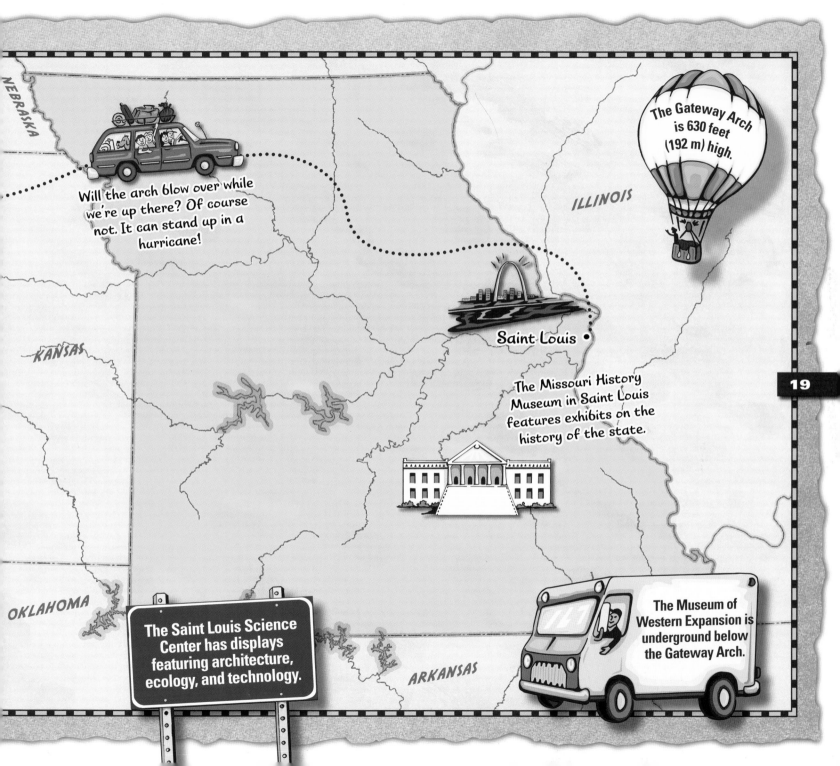

Will the arch blow over while we're up there? Of course not. It can stand up in a hurricane!

The Gateway Arch is 630 feet (192 m) high.

The Missouri History Museum in Saint Louis features exhibits on the history of the state.

The Saint Louis Science Center has displays featuring architecture, ecology, and technology.

The Museum of Western Expansion is underground below the Gateway Arch.

NEBRASKA

ILLINOIS

KANSAS

Saint Louis

OKLAHOMA

ARKANSAS

19

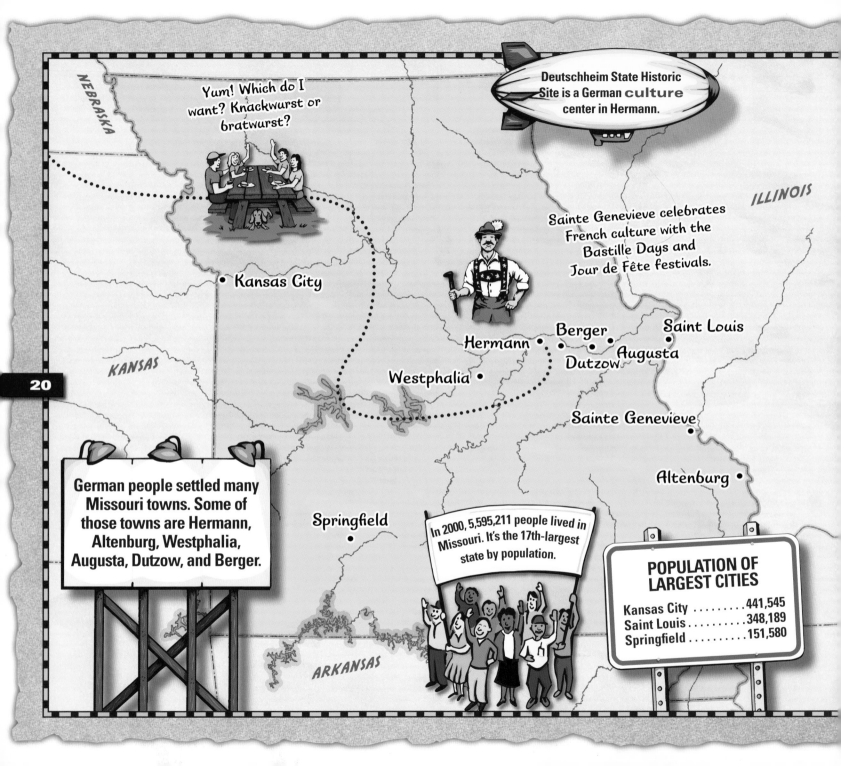

Yum! Which do I want? Knackwurst or bratwurst?

Deutschheim State Historic Site is a German **culture** center in Hermann.

Sainte Genevieve celebrates French culture with the Bastille Days and Jour de Fête festivals.

NEBRASKA

ILLINOIS

KANSAS

ARKANSAS

• Kansas City

Hermann •  • Berger  • Saint Louis
Dutzow  Augusta

Westphalia •

Sainte Genevieve •

Altenburg •

Springfield
•

German people settled many Missouri towns. Some of those towns are Hermann, Altenburg, Westphalia, Augusta, Dutzow, and Berger.

In 2000, 5,595,211 people lived in Missouri. It's the 17th-largest state by population.

**POPULATION OF LARGEST CITIES**

Kansas City . . . . . . . . . 441,545
Saint Louis . . . . . . . . . . 348,189
Springfield . . . . . . . . . . 151,580

## German Festivals in Hermann

**D**o you like sausage? Then Hermann is the place for you! This town has lots of German festivals. And they all serve plenty of sausage!

Wurstfest takes place in March. You can watch experts make sausage there. And you can fill your tummy with sausage! May is the time for Maifest. Children dress up and march in a parade. And people are selling sausages. Octoberfest is in October, of course. There you'll eat German cakes and sauerkraut. And more sausage!

Germans were among Missouri's early settlers. Many other people moved to Missouri. They came from Europe, Asia, and Spanish-speaking lands.

Costumed singers perform at a German festival in Hermann.

Kansas City holds a huge Saint Patrick's Day parade. Saint Patrick is the patron saint of Ireland. His feast day is March 17.

## Athens Battlefield and the Civil War

Imagine a **cannonball** smashing through your kitchen wall. That's what happened to a house in Athens. A cannonball shot two holes through the kitchen! You can see them, too. Just visit the Battle of Athens State Historic Site.

This battle took place during the Civil War (1861–1865). Northern and Southern states were fighting over slavery. Northerners were against using African Americans as slaves. But Southern states wanted to keep slavery.

People on both sides lived in Missouri. It was a state that allowed slavery. But Missouri joined the North in the war. After the North won, the slaves were freed.

Was that noise gunfire? Performers act out the Battle of Athens.

Wilson's Creek National Battlefield is near Springfield. It's the site of an August 10, 1861, Civil War battle.

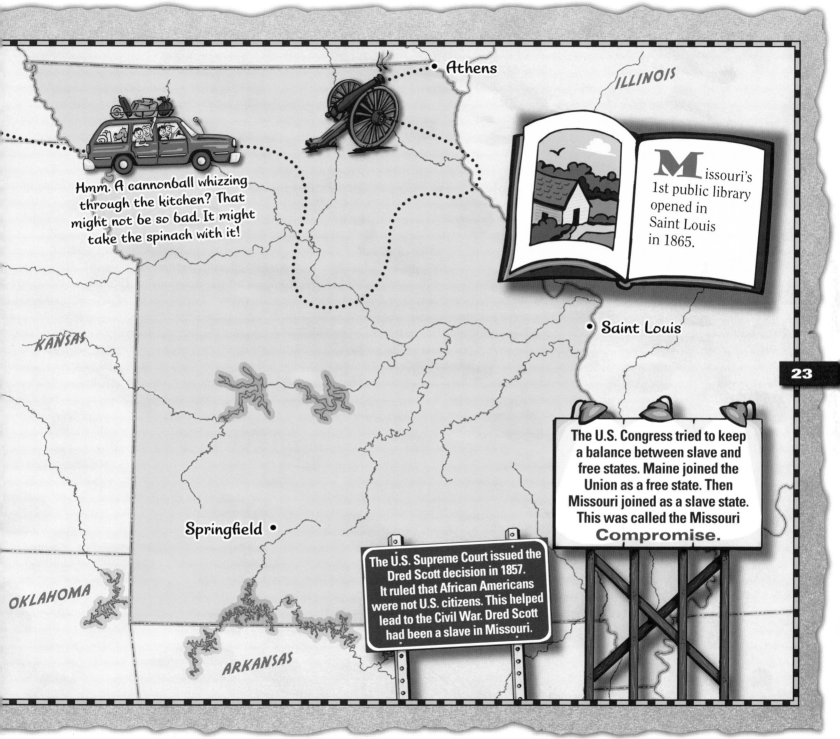

Athens

ILLINOIS

Hmm. A cannonball whizzing through the kitchen? That might not be so bad. It might take the spinach with it!

**M**issouri's 1st public library opened in Saint Louis in 1865.

KANSAS

Saint Louis

The U.S. Congress tried to keep a balance between slave and free states. Maine joined the Union as a free state. Then Missouri joined as a slave state. This was called the Missouri **Compromise.**

Springfield •

The U.S. Supreme Court issued the Dred Scott decision in 1857. It ruled that African Americans were not U.S. citizens. This helped lead to the Civil War. Dred Scott had been a slave in Missouri.

OKLAHOMA

ARKANSAS

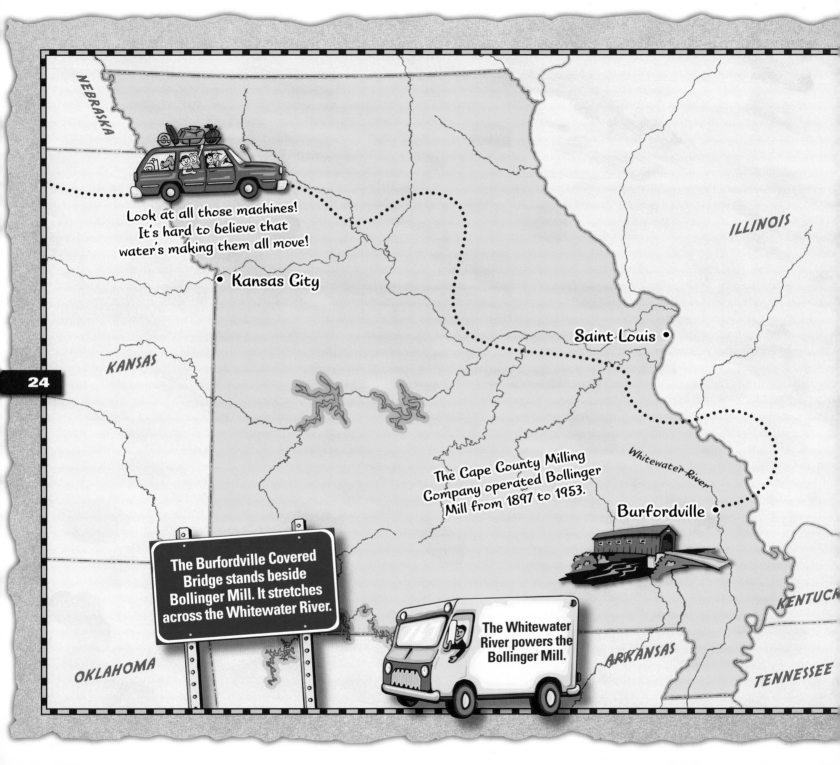

Look at all those machines! It's hard to believe that water's making them all move!

Kansas City

Saint Louis

The Cape County Milling Company operated Bollinger Mill from 1897 to 1953.

Whitewater River

Burfordville

The Burfordville Covered Bridge stands beside Bollinger Mill. It stretches across the Whitewater River.

The Whitewater River powers the Bollinger Mill.

**D**o you know what a mill is? It's an early type of factory. Mills were built beside rivers. The water turned the mill's big wheel around. The turning wheel powered the mill's machines.

Want to see a working mill? Just visit Bollinger Mill. It ground wheat into flour. It also ground corn into cornmeal. And it's still grinding away!

Flour and cornmeal were important Missouri products. So were cattle and hogs. People shipped their products to big-city markets. Saint Louis and Kansas City became trade centers. They were transportation centers, too. Goods came through on railroads and steamboats.

Cross the covered bridge and tour Bollinger Mill!

This Missouri farmer raises soybeans.

**Kirksville holds a turkey-calling contest every April.**

## Marshall's Corn Husking Championship

**A**re you a good corn husker? Then try the Missouri State Corn Husking Championship. Husking means ripping off the husk. That's the leafy covering on an ear of corn. Can you keep up?

This contest is part of the Saline County Fair. Besides husking, there's plenty to do there. You can hunt for money in a corn pile. Or you can enter the corn-throwing contest. Do you like animals? Find your favorite animal at the petting zoo.

Missourians love to celebrate their farm **traditions.** Beef cattle and hogs are the top farm products. Chickens and dairy cattle are important, too. Soybeans are the top crop. But corn's a lot more fun!

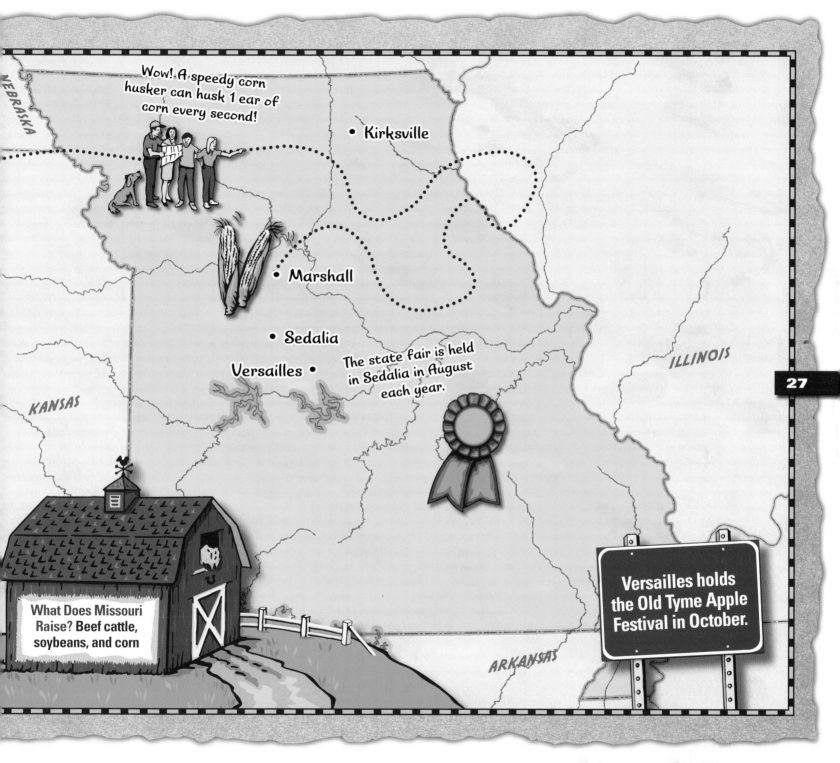

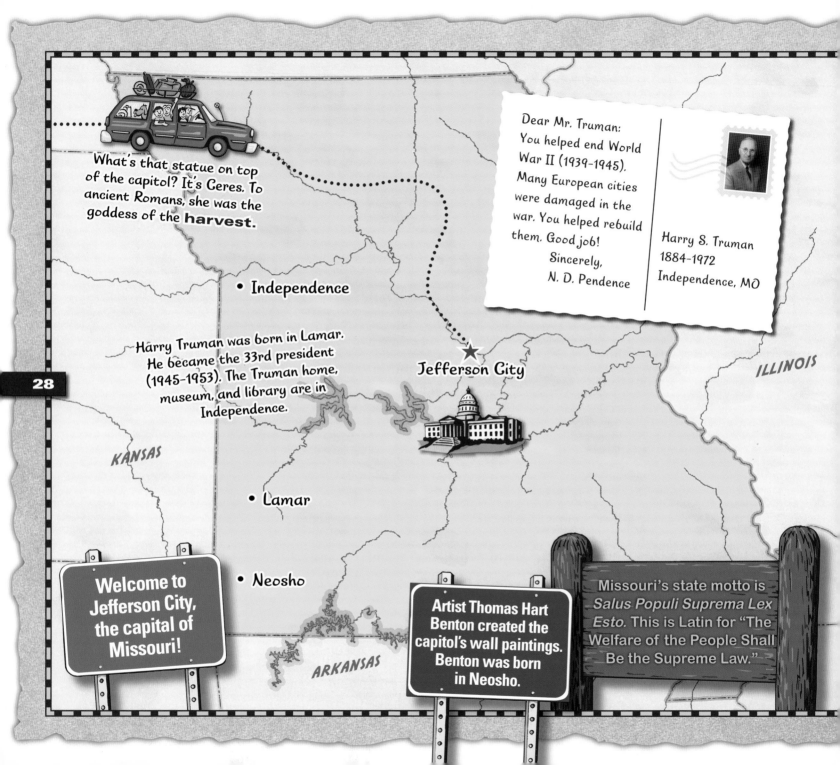

What's that statue on top of the capitol? It's Ceres. To ancient Romans, she was the goddess of the **harvest.**

Dear Mr. Truman:
You helped end World War II (1939-1945). Many European cities were damaged in the war. You helped rebuild them. Good job!
Sincerely,
N. D. Pendence

Harry S. Truman
1884-1972
Independence, MO

• Independence

Harry Truman was born in Lamar. He became the 33rd president (1945-1953). The Truman home, museum, and library are in Independence.

★ Jefferson City

ILLINOIS

KANSAS

• Lamar

• Neosho

**Welcome to Jefferson City, the capital of Missouri!**

**Artist Thomas Hart Benton created the capitol's wall paintings. Benton was born in Neosho.**

Missouri's state motto is *Salus Populi Suprema Lex Esto.* This is Latin for "The Welfare of the People Shall Be the Supreme Law."

ARKANSAS

## The State Capitol in Jefferson City

Take a tour of the state capitol. You'll get a real education. And you don't have to read a thing! There's a big room on the first floor. Step inside, and your jaw will drop. All the walls are brightly painted. They show scenes from Missouri's history.

Inside the capitol are important state government offices. Missouri's government has three branches. The General Assembly forms one branch. Its members make the state laws. The governor heads another branch. It carries out the laws. Judges make up the third branch. They decide whether laws have been broken.

Are Missouri lawmakers still awake? They work inside the capitol in Jefferson City.

In 2000, Jefferson City was Missouri's 15th-largest city.

Would you like to be a pilot? Visit Boeing's Prologue Room to learn more about airplanes.

James McDonnell founded McDonnell Aircraft Company in Saint Louis in 1939.

## Boeing's Air and Space Exhibit

Do you like airplanes and spacecraft? Then check out the Air and Space Exhibit. It's in Boeing's Prologue Room in Saint Louis. You'll see giant airplane models. You'll also see life-size models of space capsules. They're a lot like some very famous spacecraft. Why are they famous? They carried the first U.S. astronauts into space!

Farming was once Missouri's major **industry.** But new industries took over in the mid-1900s. New factories made electronics, airplanes, and other goods.

McDonnell Douglas became a huge Saint Louis company. It made aircraft for the U.S. armed forces. It also made airplanes for regular travel. Now McDonnell Douglas is part of Boeing.

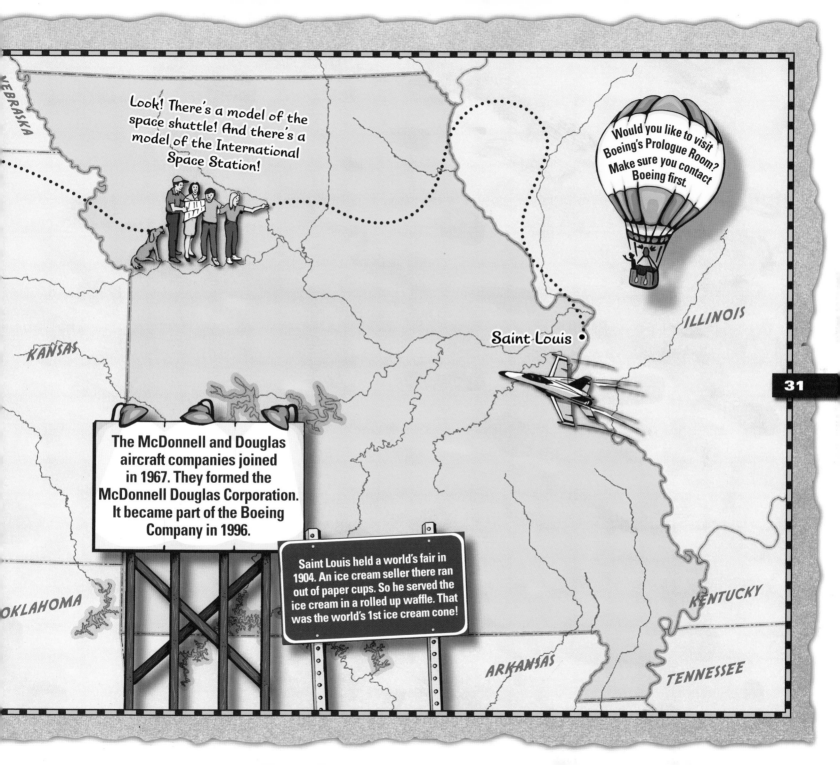

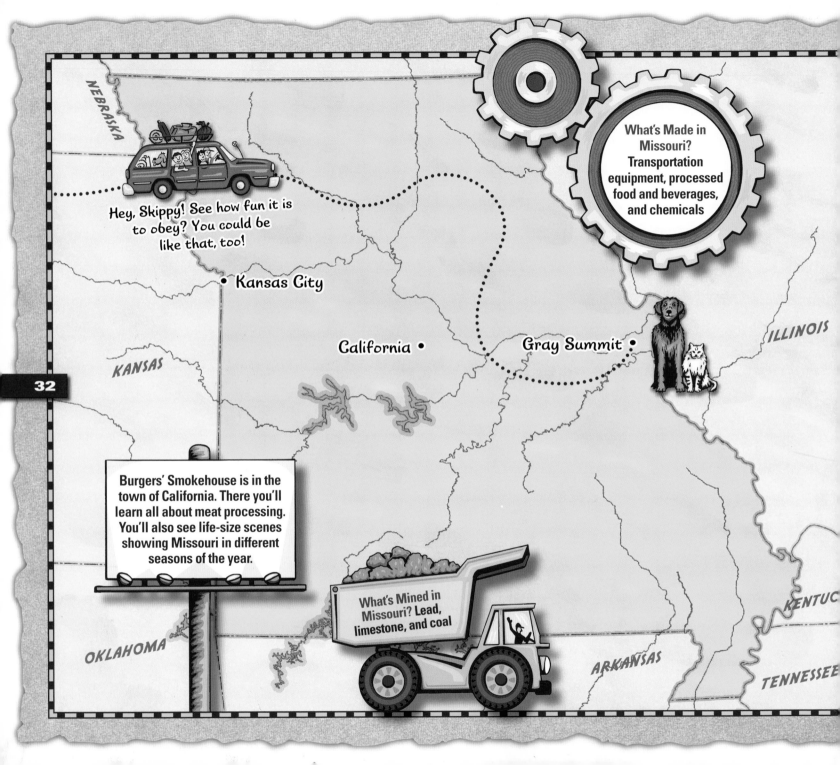

NEBRASKA

Hey, Skippy! See how fun it is to obey? You could be like that, too!

What's Made in Missouri? Transportation equipment, processed food and beverages, and chemicals

Kansas City

California •

Gray Summit •

ILLINOIS

KANSAS

Burgers' Smokehouse is in the town of California. There you'll learn all about meat processing. You'll also see life-size scenes showing Missouri in different seasons of the year.

What's Mined in Missouri? Lead, limestone, and coal

OKLAHOMA

KENTUC

ARKANSAS

TENNESSEE

## Pet Tricks at Purina Farms

The dog sits up tall. It jumps up and then rolls over. Good doggie!

You're visiting Purina Farms in Gray Summit. And you're watching a dog **obedience** show!

Purina Farms is a pet food factory. It's great fun to visit. You'll cuddle with puppies and kittens. You'll milk cows and play in the hay. And you'll learn about caring for your pet.

Missouri factories make much more than pet food. The top factory products are things that go! That means aircraft, train cars, trucks, and cars. Foods are also important factory products. That includes milk, meats, flour, and beer. Yes, and pet food, too!

Good jump, Sparky! A dog competes in a contest at Purina Farms.

Kansas City is a major center for processing meat and grain.

34

On your marks, get set, paint! Kids get messy at Hannibal's fence-painting contest.

**Mark Twain's real name was Samuel Langhorne Clemens.**

**A**re you good at painting? Try the fence-painting contest. Do you have a frog? It can enter the jumping frog contest. These are some events during Tom Sawyer Days!

Tom Sawyer was a boy in a famous book. It's called *The Adventures of Tom Sawyer.* Mark Twain, the author, grew up in Hannibal. The town celebrates Twain with Tom Sawyer Days.

Twain used real people in his books. He just changed their names. Tom may be based on Twain himself. One day, Tom had to paint a fence. He told his friends that fence painting is fun. So they finished the job for him!

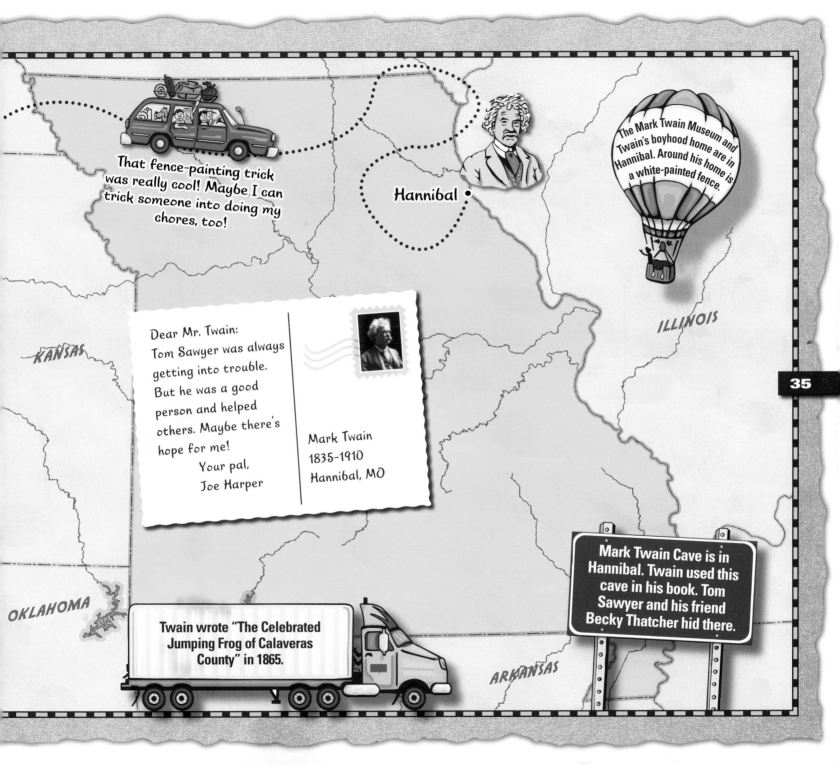

That fence-painting trick was really cool! Maybe I can trick someone into doing my chores, too!

The Mark Twain Museum and Twain's boyhood home are in Hannibal. Around his home is a white-painted fence.

Hannibal

ILLINOIS

KANSAS

Dear Mr. Twain:
Tom Sawyer was always getting into trouble. But he was a good person and helped others. Maybe there's hope for me!
Your pal,
Joe Harper

Mark Twain
1835-1910
Hannibal, MO

Mark Twain Cave is in Hannibal. Twain used this cave in his book. Tom Sawyer and his friend Becky Thatcher hid there.

OKLAHOMA

Twain wrote "The Celebrated Jumping Frog of Calaveras County" in 1865.

ARKANSAS

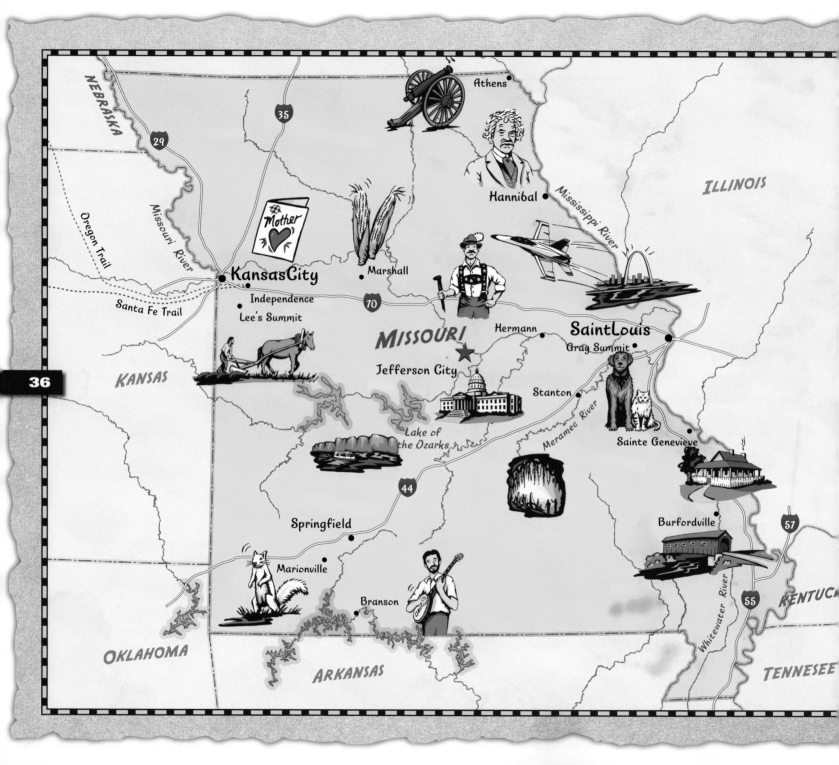

NEBRASKA

29

35

Athens

Hannibal

Mississippi River

ILLINOIS

Mother

Oregon Trail

Missouri River

KansasCity

Marshall

Independence

Santa Fe Trail

Lee's Summit

70

SaintLouis

MISSOURI

Hermann

Gray Summit

KANSAS

Jefferson City

Stanton

Meramec River

Lake of the Ozarks

Sainte Genevieve

44

Springfield

Burfordville

57

Marionville

Branson

Whitewater River

55

KENTUCK

OKLAHOMA

ARKANSAS

TENNESEE

## OUR TRIP

We visited many amazing places on our trip! We also met a lot of interesting people along the way. Look at the map on the left. Use your finger to trace all the places we have been.

**What famous outlaw hid in Meramec Caverns?** See page 7 for the answer.

**What year was the Lake of the Ozarks created?** Page 8 has the answer.

**What is Missouri's deepest cave?** See page 10 for the answer.

**Where is the International Bowling Museum?** Look on page 18 for the answer.

**Where is the state fair held each year?** Page 27 has the answer.

**What is the capital of Missouri?** Turn to page 28 for the answer.

**What was invented at the 1904 World's Fair?** Look on page 31 for the answer.

**What was Mark Twain's real name?** Turn to page 34 for the answer.

That was a great trip! We have traveled all over Missouri!

There are a few places that we didn't have time for, though. Next time, we plan to visit Hallmark Visitors' Center in Kansas City. We'll learn how greeting cards are made. If we're lucky, we'll even get to watch some artists and technicians!

More Places to Visit in Missouri

## WORDS TO KNOW

**albinos** (al-BYE-nohz) animals with white hair, light skin, and pink eyes

**arch** (ARCH) something curved like an upside-down letter *U*

**cannonball** (KAN-uhn-bawl) a big ball that's shot out of a cannon

**compromise** (KOM-pruh-mize) an agreement in which both sides get something and give up something

**culture** (KUHL-chur) a group of people's beliefs, customs, and ways of life

**harvest** (HAR-vist) gathering ripe crops; or, the crops that are gathered

**heritage** (HER-uh-tij) customs and ways of life passed down over time

**industry** (IN-duh-stree) a type of business

**missionaries** (MISH-uh-ner-eez) people who try to spread their religion in an area

**obedience** (oh-BEE-dee-uhnss) the act of obeying directions

**pioneers** (pye-uh-NEERZ) people who move into an unsettled land

**traditions** (truh-DISH-uhnz) long-held customs and ways of doing things

**tributary** (TRIB-yuh-ter-ee) a river that flows into a bigger river

Missouri covers 68,886 square miles (178,414 sq km). It's the 18th-largest state in size.

# STATE SYMBOLS

**State American folk dance:** Square dance

**State animal:** Missouri mule

**State aquatic animal:** Paddlefish

**State bird:** Bluebird

**State fish:** Channel catfish

**State flower:** White hawthorn blossom

**State fossil:** Crinoid

**State insect:** Honeybee

**State mineral:** Galena

**State musical instrument:** Fiddle

**State rock:** Mozarkite

**State tree:** Flowering dogwood

**State tree nut:** Eastern black walnut

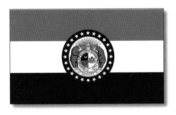

State flag

State seal

# STATE SONG

## "Missouri Waltz"

*Words by James R. Shannon, music by John V. Eppel*

Hush-a-bye, ma baby, slumbertime is comin' soon;
Rest yo' head upon my breast while Mommy hums a tune;
The sandman is callin' where shadows are fallin',
While the soft breezes sigh as in days long gone by.

Way down in Missouri where I heard this melody,
When I was a little child upon my Mommy's knee;
The old folks were hummin'; their banjos were strummin';
So sweet and low.

Strum, strum, strum, strum, strum,
Seems I hear those banjos playin' once again,
Hum, hum, hum, hum, hum,
That same old plaintive strain.

Hear that mournful melody,
It just haunts you the whole day long,
And you wander in dreams back to Dixie, it seems,
When you hear that old time song.

Hush-a-bye ma baby, go to sleep on Mommy's knee,
Journey back to Dixieland in dreams again with me;
It seems like your Mommy is there once again,
And the old folks were strummin' that same old refrain.

Way down in Missouri where I learned this lullaby,
When the stars were blinkin' and the moon was climbin' high,
Seems I hear voices low, as in days long ago,
Singin' hush-a-bye.

# FAMOUS PEOPLE

Altman, Robert (1925– ), film director

Bacharach, Burt (1928– ), composer

Baker, Josephine (1906–1975), entertainer

Berra, Yogi (1925– ), baseball player

Carver, George Washington (1864–1943), educator, botanist

Cronkite, Walter (1916– ), television broadcast journalist

Eliot, T. S. (1888–1965), poet

Hubble, Edwin (1889–1953), astronomer

Hughes, Langston (1902–1967), author

James, Jesse (1847–1882), outlaw

Lester, Julius (1939– ), children's author

Price, Vincent (1911–1993), actor

Pulitzer, Joseph (1847–1911), journalist and publisher

Rogers, Ginger (1911–1995), dancer and actor

Ross, Nellie Tayloe (1876–1977), 1st woman governor of a state

Truman, Harry S. (1884–1972), 33rd U.S. president

Twain, Mark (pen name of Samuel Clemens) (1835–1910), author

Van Dyke, Dick (1925– ), comedic actor

Wilder, Laura Ingalls (1867–1957), children's author

Wilkins, Roy (1901–1981), civil rights leader

# TO FIND OUT MORE

## At the Library
Brown, Don. *American Boy: The Adventures of Mark Twain*. Boston: Houghton Mifflin Company, 2003.

Gaines, Ann Graham. *Harry S. Truman: Our Thirty-Third President*. Chanhassen, Minn.: The Child's World, 2002.

Lago, Mary Ellen. *Missouri*. New York: Children's Press, 2003.

Young, Judy, and Ross B. Young (illustrator). *S Is for Show Me: A Missouri Alphabet*. Chelsea, Mich.: Sleeping Bear Press, 2001.

## On the Web
Visit our home page for lots of links about Missouri:
*http://www.childsworld.com/links*

Note to Parents, Teachers, and Librarians: We routinely verify our Web links to make sure they are safe, active sites—so encourage your readers to check them out!

## Places to Visit or Contact
**Missouri Division of Tourism**
301 W. High Street
PO Box 1055
Jefferson City, MO 65102
573/751-4133
*For more information about traveling in Missouri*

**Missouri Historical Society**
PO Box 11940
Saint Louis, MO 63112-0040
314/454-3187
*For more information about the history of Missouri*

# INDEX

*The Adventures of Tom Sawyer* (Mark Twain), 34
Air and Space Exhibit, 30, *30*
American Indians, 14
American Plunge, 10, *10*
animals, 12, 13, 18, 25, 26, 33
Athens, 22

Bagnell Dam, 8
Battle of Athens State Historic Site, 22
Benton, Thomas Hart, 28
birds, 12, 13
bluebird (state bird), 12
bobwhites. *See* quails.
Boeing Company, 30, 31
Bollinger Mill, 24, 25, *25*
borders, 6
Branson, 9, 11
Burfordville, 24, 25
Burfordville Covered Bridge, 24
Burgers' Smokehouse, 32

Cape County Milling Company, 24
Carver, George Washington, 9
caves, 6, *6*, 7, 10, 35
Civil War, 22, *22*, 23
Clark, William, 17
Clemens, Samuel Langhorn, 34
climate, 7

Diamond, 9
Dred Scott case, 23

elevation, 7

farming, 6, 17, 26, *26*, 30
flowering dogwood (state tree), 12
French explorers, 14
French Heritage Festival, 14, *14*
Frisco Steam Train, 10
fur trade, 14

Gateway Arch, 18, *18*
General Assembly, 29
Germans, 20, 21, *21*
Geyser Gulch, 10
governors, 29

Hannibal, 34, 35
Harry S. Truman Reservoir, 6
Hermann, 21

ice cream cones, 31
Independence, 17
industry, 30, 33
International Bowling Museum, 18

Jefferson City, 28, 29
Joliet, Louis, 15
judges, 29

Kansas City, 20, 21, 25, 33
Kirksville, 26

Laclède, Pierre, 14
Lake of the Ozarks, 6, 8, 9, *9*
landforms, 6, *6*, 7, 10, 35
landmarks, 18, *18*, 28, 29, *29*
Lee's Summit, 17
Lewis, Meriwether, 17
livestock, 25, 26, 33

Maifest, 21
major cities, 13, 18, 20, 21, 22, 25, 30, 31, 33
marine life, 13
Marionville, 13
Mark Twain Cave, 35
Marmaros, 11
Marquette, Jacques, 15
Marshall, 26
Marvel Cave, 10
McDonnell Douglas Corporation, 30, 31
McDonnell, James, 30
Meramec Caverns, 6, *6*, 7
missionaries, 14
Mississippi River, 6, 14, 15
Missouri Compromise, 23
Missouri River, 6, 15
Missouri State Corn Husking Championship, 26
Missouri Town 1855, 17, *17*
music, 9, 14, *14*

National Frontier Trails Center, 17
national parks, 12
natural resources, 26, *26*
Neosho, 28

Octoberfest, 21
Old Tyme Apple Festival, 27
Oregon Trail, 17
Osage River, 8
Ozark cavefish, 13
Ozark Cavefish National Wildlife Refuge, 13
Ozark Mountains, 6, 13

pioneers, 17
places of interest, 6, *6*, 7, 9, 10, *10*, 11, 13, 16, 17, *17*, 18, *18*, 21, *21*, 22, *22*, 24, 25, *25*, 26, 27, 28, 29, *29*, 30, *30*, 32, 33, *33*
plant life, 12, 26
Pony Express National Museum, 16
population, 20
pralines, 15
Prologue Room, 30, *30*
Purina Farms, 33, *33*

quails, 13

Saint Joseph, 16
Saint Louis, 18, 20, 25, 30, 31
Saint Louis Science Center, 18, 19
Saint Patrick's Day, 21
Sainte Genevieve, 14
Saline County Fair, 26
Santa Fe Trail, 17
Scott, Dred, 23
settlers, 17, 20, 21

Silver Dollar City, 9, 10, *10*, 11
slavery, 22, 23
soybeans, 26
spacecraft, 30
sports, 8, 9, *9*
Springfield, 13, 20, 22
Stage Curtain, 7
state bird, 12
state capital, 28
state capitol, 28, 29, *29*
state flower, 12
state government, 29
state motto, 28
state nickname, 4
state tree, 12
statehood, 16, 23

Tom Sawyer Days, 34, *34*
Truman, Harry S., 28, *28*
Twain, Mark, 34, 35, *35*

Versailles, 27

WaterWorks Waterboggan, 10
white hawthorn blossom (state flower), 12
white squirrels, 13
Whitewater River, 24
Wilson's Creek National Battlefield, 22
World War II, 28
Wurstfest, 21

Bye, Show-Me State.
We had a great time.
We'll come back soon!